The Bible Alphabet

EXPLORING THE WONDERS OF THE BIBLE FROM A-Z

Lee Ann B. Marino, Ph.D., D.Min., D.D.

The Bible Alphabet

Exploring the Wonders of the Bible from A-Z

LEE ANN B MARINO, PH.D., D.MIN., D.D.

Published by:

Burning Bush Books

(An imprint of The Righteous Pen Publications Group)

www.righteouspenpublications.com

ISBN: 1-940197-53-8
13-Digit: 978-1-940197-53-1

Printed in the United States of America.

A Note To The Grown-Ups Who Read This Book With Children

> *Train up a child in the way he should go,*
> *And even when he is old*
> *he will not depart from it.*
> *(Proverbs 22:6)*

In years past, reading the Scriptures was a powerful means of Christian instruction within the home, the school, and even the church school setting. With limited reading choices, the reading the Bible served not only for the purpose of faith and guidance, but also as one of the most basic books for educational and creative purposes. Parents, grandparents, guardians, teachers, and ministers spent time reading the Bible to children, whether as part of family devotional or prayer time, reading class, or Scriptural instruction. Such established a strong cornerstone within Christian families, schools, and churches to lay the foundation for strong Scriptural devotion as children matured into adulthood.

Today, with a plethora of literary choices for children, Bible reading is sometimes regarded as unnecessary for children, even in some Christian circles. There are some who even suggest that reading the Bible can harm a child. While I do believe certain translations and passages are more appropriate for children than others, the notion that Bible reading will harm a child is absurd. Not only will reading the Bible a child cause them no harm, it will help to edify them and lay their foundation for faith into adulthood.

I do acknowledge that reading the Bible with twenty-first century children can present a challenge. Today's children are used to constant stimulation with video games, movies, fast-paced action violence on television, and cartoons, all distractions parents of yesteryear did not compete with when it came time to read the Scriptures. Many children, especially young children, can find the size of most Bibles daunting, with small type, archaic or formal language, many pages, and few (if any) pictures. While "children's Bibles" are helpful to a certain age, the paraphrases of text found within them often express the author's perspectives on the meaning of passages rather than giving solid, clear Biblical stories in an easily understood manner. When faced with Bible reading today, many parents and instructors relent to society's conditioning of children, and buy Bible stories in cartoon-form on DVD or leave Scripture education up to skits or methods of entertainment.

In light of the world's message to children: "You need constant entertainment," taking the time to read the Scriptures with children is all the more important. Children need to learn there are things in this world worth taking the time to read, that important things aren't always showy or fast-paced, and that we make time for what matters in life. Faith is a process by which we trust God for what we cannot now see, and it isn't God's job to constantly entertain us. Much of the time, He asks us to trust and believe in Him through difficult times and hard circumstances that we'd rather not encounter. Bible reading with children establishes the foundation for right living, as they learn God comes first and we must make learning His Word a priority in this life.

Reading the Bible also helps develop literary skills within children. It is a known fact that reading to children helps with reading abilities, word identification, proper pronunciation of words, sentence structure, and reading comprehension. Not only is it a good way to spend time and connect with a child, it is an educational grounding for them as well.

The Bible Alphabet serves as a starting point for Bible reading with young children. I remember teaching a fifth grade religion class about twenty years ago and seeing how responsive children were, even as old as ten and eleven, with associations presented in an easy-to-understand manner. This precept of associations is the concept behind this book. For every letter of the alphabet, I have found a Bible person or place and written a short rhyme relating to the person or place. Along with that rhyme, you will find a Bible passage, no more than three verses in length, relating to the person or place. This creates an association for the child between the Bible person or place and the passage of the Bible where it is found, making the characters easy to remember and the verses accessible instead of daunting. Through association, the next natural step is Bible reading, perhaps the chapter or surrounding verses of the passage mentioned in the book.

The illustrations of this book also stand as a modern-day, updated version of classic paintings, photo-edited for relatability with children, of major Bible figures and events. I decided to fill this book with updated versions of classic images to help foster education, as well as to provide the classic beauty that has long been a part of Bible history, from the past to the present. At the end of this book, you will find a complete list of all the artwork used, the original artists, and the year in which it was first created.

The Bible is a fascinating book, filled with heroes and villains, sinners and saints, people and places, decisions and choices, cause and effect, and, above all, God's communication with humanity and His salvation merited through His Son, Jesus Christ. It is no accident it has been called, "The greatest story ever told." As it has fascinated generations past, God's Word can and will fascinate this current generation of people through His power and revelation.

A is for Adam,

human father of all;
and on account of an apple,
led us into the fall.

And Jehovah God took the man, and put him into the garden of Eden to dress it and to keep it. And Jehovah God commanded the man, saying, Of every tree of the garden thou mayest freely eat: but of the tree of the knowledge of good and evil, thou shalt not eat of it: for in the day that thou eatest thereof thou shalt surely die.
(Genesis 2:15-17)

B is for Babel,

a tower so high!
God came and destroyed it,
and then it was nigh!

So Jehovah scattered them abroad from thence upon the face of all the earth: and they left off building the city. Therefore was the name of it called Babel; because Jehovah did there confound the language of all the earth: and from thence did Jehovah scatter them abroad upon the face of all the earth.
(Genesis 11:8-9)

C is for Cana,

where they ran out of wine.
Jesus transformed the water,
and guests said it was fine.

And when the ruler of the feast tasted the water now become wine, and knew not whence it was (but the servants that had drawn the water knew), the ruler of the feast calleth the bridegroom, and saith unto him, Every man setteth on first the good wine; and when men have drunk freely, then that which is worse: thou hast kept the good wine until now."
(John 2:9-10)

D is for David,

a king, strong and bold;
who led a Bible people,
in ancient days of old.

Then all Israel gathered themselves to David unto Hebron, saying, Behold, we are thy bone and thy flesh. In times past, even when Saul was king, it was thou that leddest out and broughtest in Israel: and Jehovah thy God said unto thee, Thou shalt be shepherd of My people Israel, and thou shalt be prince over My people Israel. So all the elders of Israel came to the king to Hebron; and David made a covenant with them in Hebron before Jehovah; and they anointed David king over Israel, according to the word of Jehovah by Samuel.
(1 Chronicles 11:1-3)

E is for Esther,

whose insights so keen
gave her boldness and
courage,
and then she became queen.

Then Mordecai bade them return answer unto Esther, Think not with thyself that thou shalt escape in the king's house, more than all the Jews. For if thou altogether holdest thy peace at this time, then will relief and deliverance arise to the Jews from another place, but thou and thy father's house will perish: and who knoweth whether thou art not come to the kingdom for such a time as this? Then Esther bade them return answer unto Mordecai, Go, gather together all the Jews that are present in Shushan, and fast ye for me, and neither eat nor drink three days, night or day: I also and my maidens will fast in like manner; and so will I go in unto the king, which is not according to the law: and if I perish, I perish."

(Esther 4:13-16)

F is for Fortunatus,

who with grace did supply
a spiritual refreshing,
which one cannot buy.

And I rejoice at the coming of Stephanas and Fortunatus and Achaicus: for that which was lacking on your part they supplied. For they refreshed my spirit and yours: acknowledge ye therefore them that are such.
(1 Corinthians 16:17-18)

G is for Gabriel,

who to Mary did say,
a most wonderful message:
"The Lord is with you,
always!"

Now in the sixth month the angel Gabriel was sent from God unto a city of Galilee, named Nazareth, to a virgin betrothed to a man whose name was Joseph, of the house of David; and the virgin's name was Mary. And he came in unto her, and said, Hail, thou that art highly favored, the Lord is with thee.
(Luke 1:26-28)

H is for Hephzibah,

"Beloved daughter of God!"
And as God's holy nation,
to hear that won't be odd!

ISAIAH II Chap. 6 & 7

"Thou shalt also be a crown of beauty in the hand of Jehovah, and a royal diadem in the hand of thy God. Thou shalt no more be termed Forsaken; neither shall thy land any more be termed Desolate: but thou shalt be called Hephzi-bah, and thy land Beulah; for Jehovah delighteth in thee, and thy land shall be married."
(Isaiah 62:3-4)

I is for Israel,

which wandered around
in the wilderness for forty
years,
and camped on the ground.

And thou shalt remember all the way which Jehovah thy God hath led thee these forty years in the wilderness, that He might humble thee, to prove thee, to know what was in thy heart, whether thou wouldest keep His commandments, or not. And He humbled thee, and suffered thee to hunger, and fed thee with manna, which thou knewest not, neither did thy fathers know; that He might make thee know that man doth not live by bread only, but by everything that proceedeth out of the mouth of Jehovah doth man live. Thy raiment waxed not old upon thee, neither did thy foot swell, these forty years. And thou shalt consider in thy heart, that, as a man chasteneth his son, so Jehovah thy God chasteneth thee.
(Deuteronomy 8:2-5)

J is for Jesus,

our Savior is He;
and for our redemption
was hung on a tree.

And Pilate wrote a title also, and put it on the cross. And there was written, JESUS OF NAZARETH, THE KING OT THE JEWS. This title therefore read many of the Jews, for the place where Jesus was crucified was nigh to the city; and it was written in Hebrew, and in Latin, and in Greek...When Jesus therefore had received the vinegar, He said, It is finished: and He bowed His head, and gave up His spirit.
(John 19:19-20,30)

K is for Kadmiel

and sons to supervise
the building of God's house,
whose actions were quite
wise.

Then stood Jeshua with his sons and his brethren, Kadmiel and his sons, the sons of Judah, together, to have the oversight of the workmen in the house of God: the sons of Henadad, with their sons and their brethren the Levites.
(Ezra 3:9)

L is for Lois

whose spiritual faith and
power
was a testament unto
Timothy
and God's servants to this
hour.

Having been reminded of the unfeigned faith that is in thee; which dwelt first in thy grandmother Lois, and thy mother Eunice; and, I am persuaded, in thee also.
(2 Timothy 1:5)

M is for Mary,

whose Son is quite well:
our Lord and our Savior,
and our Emmanuel.

Now all this is come to pass, that it might be fulfilled which was spoken by the Lord through the prophet, saying, Behold, the virgin shall be with child, and shall bring forth a son, And they shall call his name Immanuel; which is, being interpreted, God with us.
– Matthew 1:22-23

$\mathfrak{N}$ is for Noah,

whose command from above
was to sail in an ark
and then send out a dove.

And he stayed yet other seven days; and again he sent forth the dove out of the ark; and the dove came in to him at eventide; and, lo, in her mouth an olive-leaf plucked off: so Noah knew that the waters were abated from off the earth. And he stayed yet other seven days, and sent forth the dove; and she returned not again unto him any more.
(Genesis 8:11-12)

Ois for Ophir,

a land to mine the gold
to send back to King
Solomon
to make God's temple bright
and bold.

And Hiram sent in the navy his servants, shipmen that had knowledge of the sea, with the servants of Solomon. And they came to Ophir, and fetched from thence gold, four hundred and twenty talents, and brought it to king Solomon.
(1 Kings 9:27-28)

P is for Philip,
who by an angel was led
to preach the Gospel to an
eunuch,
and there God's Word was
read.

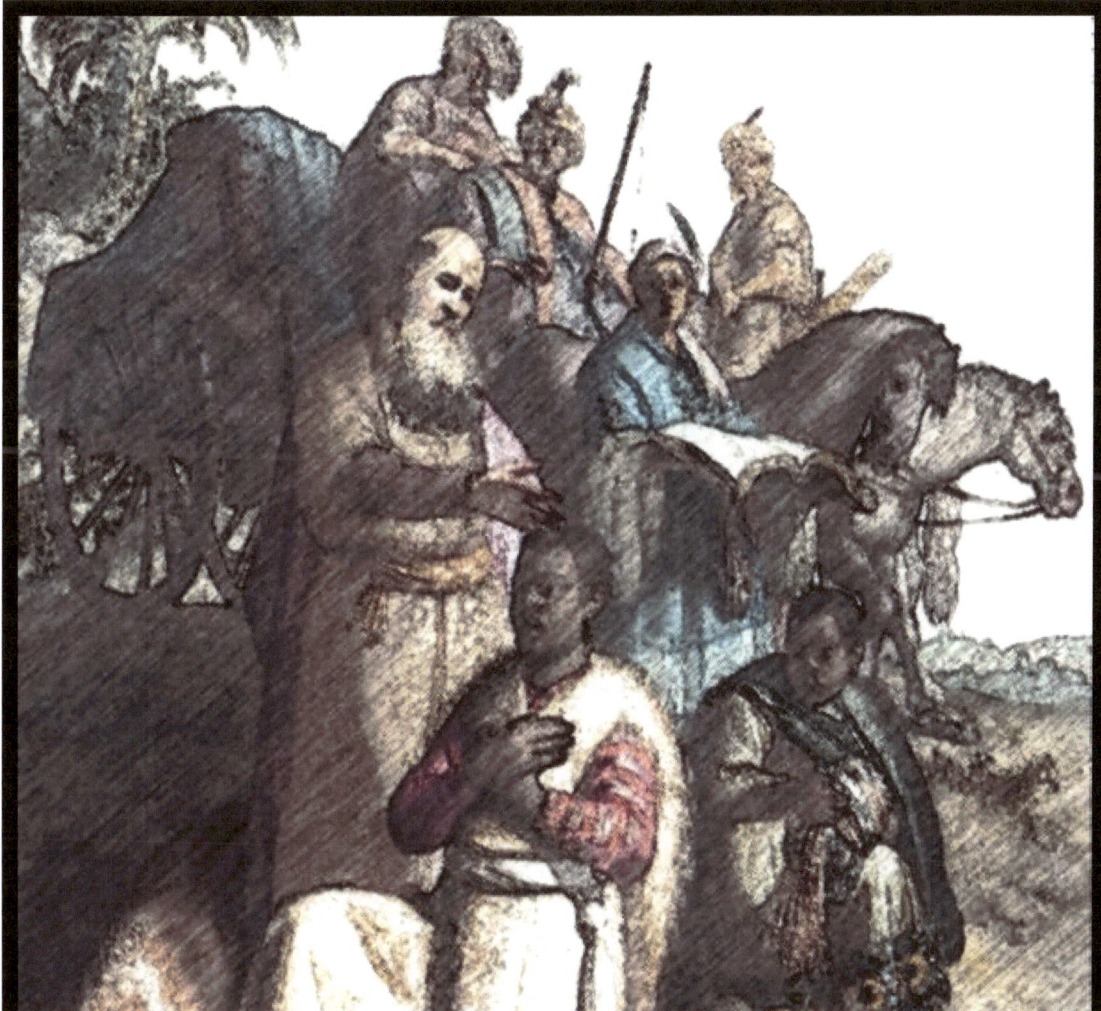

"But an angel of the Lord spake unto Philip, saying, Arise, and go toward the south unto the way that goeth down from Jerusalem unto Gaza: the same is desert. And he arose and went: and behold, a man of Ethiopia, a eunuch of great authority under Candace, queen of the Ethiopians, who was over all her treasure, who had come to Jerusalem to worship; and he was returning and sitting in his chariot, and was reading the prophet Isaiah."

(Acts 8:26-28)

Q is for Quartus,
his greetings did send
with love to the brethren,
for he was their friend.

Gaius my host, and of the whole church, saluteth you. Erastus the treasurer of the city saluteth you, and Quartus the brother. (Romans 16:23)

R is for Rahab,

who took in the spies.
She did what was righteous,
and had faith in God's eyes.

And in like manner was not also Rahab the harlot justified by works, in that she received the messengers, and sent them out another way? For as the body apart from the spirit is dead, even so faith apart from works is dead.
(James 2:25-26)

S is for Sheba,

the queen of which came
to hear Solomon's wisdom,
and was never the same.

And she said to the king, It was a true report that I heard in mine own land of thine acts, and of thy wisdom. Howbeit I believed not the words, until I came, and mine eyes had seen it: and, behold, the half was not told me; thy wisdom and prosperity exceed the fame which I heard. Happy are thy men, happy are these thy servants, that stand continually before thee, and that hear thy wisdom.
(1 Kings 10:6-8)

$\mathfrak{T}$ is for Thomas,

a doubter was he;
who would not believe in
Jesus,
unless he could touch and
see.

But Thomas, one of the twelve, called Didymus, was not with them when Jesus came. The other disciples therefore said unto him, We have seen the Lord. But he said unto them, Except I shall see in His hands the print of the nails, and put my hand into His side, I will not believe.
(John 20:24-25)

U is for Uz,

where Job lived upright.
Despite Satan's temptations,
he knew God's ways are
right.

There was a man in the land of Uz, whose name was Job; and that man was perfect and upright, and one that feared God, and turned away from evil.
(Job 1:1)

V is for Vashti,

who had no remorse. . .
She ignored the king's
command,
and then got a divorce.

But the queen Vashti refused to come at the king's commandment by the chamberlains: therefore was the king very wroth, and his anger burned in him...If it please the king, let there go forth a royal commandment from him, and let it be written among the laws of the Persians and the Medes, that it be not altered, that Vashti come no more before king Ahasuerus; and let the king give her royal estate unto another that is better than she.
(Esther 1:12,19)

W is for Wise Men,

who came from afar
to worship the child Jesus,
by following a star.

And they, having heard the king, went their way; and lo, the star, which they saw in the east, went before them, till it came and stood over where the young child was. And when they saw the star, they rejoiced with exceeding great joy. And they came into the house and saw the young child with Mary His mother; and they fell down and worshipped Him; and opening their treasures they offered unto Him gifts, gold and frankincense and myrrh.

(Matthew 2:9-11)

X is for Xerxes

in abundance and health,
who held a great banquet
to display all of his wealth.

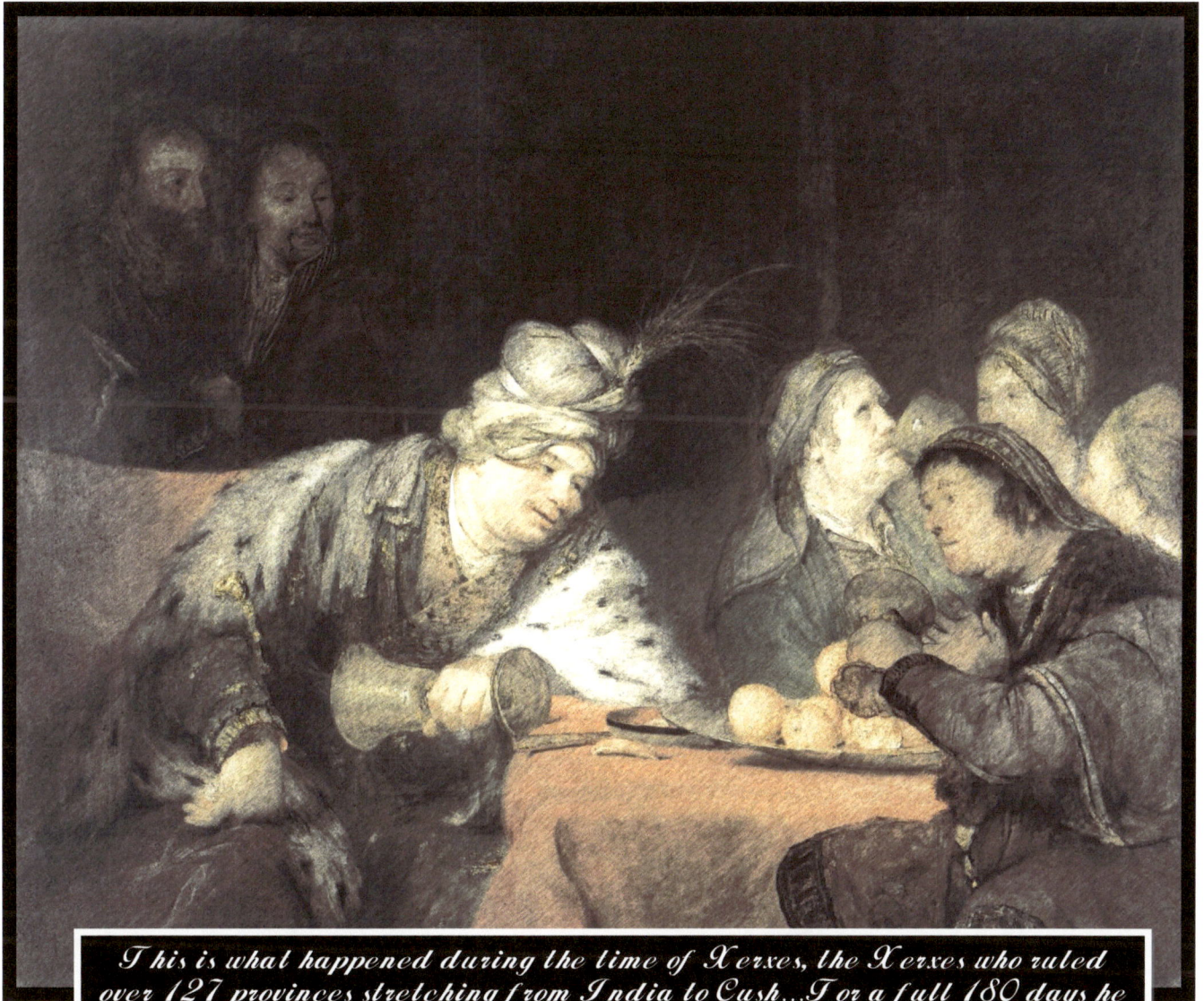

This is what happened during the time of Xerxes, the Xerxes who ruled over 127 provinces stretching from India to Cush...For a full 180 days he displayed the vast wealth of his kingdom and the splendor and glory of his majesty. When these days were over, the king gave a banquet, lasting seven days, in the enclosed garden of the king's palace, for all the people from the least to the greatest, who were in the citadel of Susa.
(Esther 1:1,4-5, NIV)

$\mathfrak{Y}$ is for Young Men,
many visions to see:
from God's spiritual
outpouring
in the Last Days, it shall be!

And it shall come to pass afterward, that I will pour out My Spirit upon all flesh; and your sons and your daughters shall prophesy, your old men shall dream dreams, your young men shall see visions: and also upon the servants and upon the handmaids in those days will I pour out My Spirit.
(Joel 2:28-29)

Z is for Zephaniah,

who told of a day
when the Messiah will come,
and put all evil away.

I will gather them that sorrow for the solemn assembly, who were of thee; to whom the burden upon her was a reproach. Behold, at that time I will deal with all them that afflict thee; and I will save that which is lame, and gather that which was driven away; and I will make them a praise and a name, whose shame hath been in all the earth.
(Zephaniah 3:18-19)

Classical Works of Art Updated for This Book

- *Adam and Eve* by Hendrick Goltzius (1613)
- *The "Little" Tower of Babel* by Pieter Bruegel the Elder (1563)
- *The Marriage Feast at Cana* by Bartolome Esteban Murillo (1675)
- *King David in Prayer* by Pieter de Grebber (c. 1637)
- *Esther and Mordechai Writing Letters to the Jews* by Aert de Gelder (1675)
- *Three Apostles with Scepter, Scimitar, and Cross*, Anonymous (15th Century)
- *Angel Gabriel Announcing to Mary that she is with Child* by Paolo de Matteis (1712)
- *Peaceable Kingdom* by Edward Hicks (1833)
- *The Tabernacle in the Wilderness*, Holman Bible (1890)
- *Apelles Pintando Campaspe* by Francesco Trevisani (1720)
- *Rebuilding the Wall of Jerusalem under Nehemiah* by William Brassey Hole (c. 1910)
- *Timothy and Lois* by Willem Drost (1650s)
- *The Virgin of the Grapes* by Pierre Mignard (1640s)
- *La Creation*, in Mosaique in Venise, Basilique Saint-Marc (1215-1230)
- *The Holy of Holies*, Holman Bible (1890)
- *The Baptism of the Eunuch* by Rembrandt (1626)

- *Apostle Paul Writing His Epistles* by Valentin de Boulogne (17th century)
- *Rahab and the Emissaries of Joshua*, Unknown (17th Century)
- *The Legendary Queen of Sheba and her Iconic Visit with King Solomon*, ancient origins
- *The Incredulity of Saint Thomas* by Caravaggio (1603)
- *Job Restored to Prosperity* by Laurent de La Hyre (1648)
- *Vashti Deposed* by Earnest Normand (1890)
- *Journey of the Magi* by James Tissot (1902)
- *The Banquet of Ahasuerus* by Aert de Gelder (1680s)
- *Outpouring of the Holy Spirit* by El Greco (1604-1614)
- *Ascension of Christ* by Dosso Dossi (16th Century)

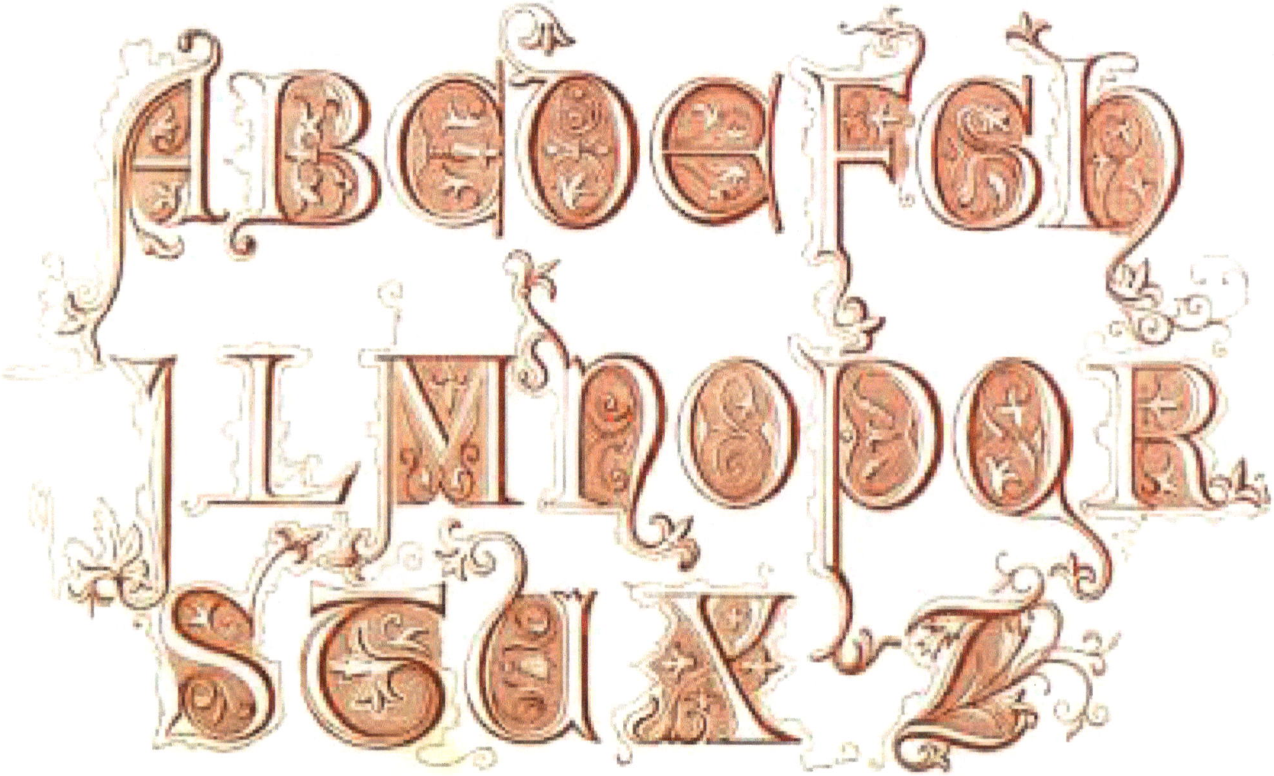
ABCDEFGH
ILMNOPQR
STUXZ

About the Author

Lee Ann B. Marino, Ph.D., D.Min., D.D., is a full-time minister, author, professor, editor, and publisher. She has been involved with Christian ministry for over 25 years and serves as a licensed and ordained minister of the Gospel, serving in her own ministry, Sanctuary Apostolic Fellowship Empowerment (SAFE) Ministries. She is also founder and Overseer of Sanctuary International Fellowship Tabernacle (SIFT) in Charlotte, North Carolina and The Sanctuary Network, and Chancellor of Apostolic Covenant Theological Seminary (ACTS). Within the Kingdom of God, Dr. Marino serves in the office of apostle. She works as a theologian specializing in queer and feminist theology, with concentrations in pneumatology, leadership development, Ephesians 4:11 ministry, ministry startup development, conceptual theology, and apostolic theology. She is host of the top 20 percentile *Kingdom Now* podcast and also serves as Chancellor for Apostolic Covenant Theological Seminary.

Dr. Marino has spent nearly 30 years in Christian education, from elementary school all the way through to postgraduate education. She is proud to stand as the author of curriculum, over 35 books on various theological and spiritual topics (including five Amazon bestsellers), and as a long-time instructor and pioneer in the field of Pentecostal Christian education, seminary, women's study, queer theology, and apostolic theological study.

Known to those she works with as spiritual mom, teacher, leader, confidant, and devoted friend, Dr. Marino continues to grow, transform, and change, receiving new teaching, revelation, and insight into this thing we call "ministry." Through years of pressing, seeking, and spiritual growth, Dr. Marino stands as herself, here to present what God has given to her for any who have an ear to hear. Her main website is www.kingdompowernow.org.

www.ingramcontent.com/pod-product-compliance
Lightning Source LLC
LaVergne TN
LVHW072129070426
835513LV00002B/38